I0475990

Short Steps To Improve Your Credit

By: Larry Mitchell

Table of Contents

Chapter 1 – Where To Begin

The first step that you should take to repair your credit is to find out where your credit stands. You can look up your credit report for free on a website called Credit Karma. The website address for them is www.creditkarma.com. This website allows you to take a quick look at your credit report for no charge. This will give you a general overview of your credit. This website only shows one major credit bureau, Transunion. However, if you want a more in-depth look at your credit report, then usually this is offered at other places and there is a fee charged for this.

There are a few different websites that offer your credit reports in which you can view your credit report in greater detail. One of those sites is called Identity Guard. Their web address is www.identityguard.com. This company allows you to see your credit report in detail from all three major credit bureaus. They also offer credit monitoring services and identity theft protection. You can also get your detailed credit report from the major credit bureaus directly. The three major credit bureaus are Experian, Equifax and TransUnion.

Before we move forward, let's take a look at what's involved in a credit report. Your credit report is simply a collection of data that shows your financial history with creditors. It shows the details on your loans, credit cards and other credit items. It also shows other items such as bankruptcies, liens, judgments and payment history. The payment history shows how many times you've been late making a payment, any past due amounts and other details about your payment history. These are some of the items that lenders look at when viewing your credit report.

Imagine yourself as a lender. If you had a hundred thousand dollars to loan out and you had to choose between two people to loan it to, who would you lend it to? Let's take a look at the two different people. Person A is someone who has good payment history, a low amount of debt and they use a low percentage of their credit limits. They show responsible credit history. Person B has been late on several bills, they max out all of their credit card limits and they have collection items on their credit. Would you lend your money to Person A or Person B? The answer would be Person A. This person shows better history. When you put yourself into the shoes of a lender, this will help you to better understand how to improve your credit.

There are some other factors to consider when you're ready to repair your credit. If you have bad credit already, then there's one mistake that you want to avoid. Don't immediately pay off your bad debt. The first thing that you should do is establish good payment history. Secured credit cards are a great way to help establish good payment history if you don't have any already.

Here is the reason that you should focus on establishing good credit before paying off your bad credit. If you pay off all of your bad credit without having good credit working for you at the same time, then you will not have anything positive working for you once the bad credit is paid off. Your history will only show the bad credit history. Essentially your credit will have no positive movement working for you.   Your credit score will not improve and it will show that you had bad debt that you took care of. It will not show that you are trustworthy again.   Think about it. It does not make sense to spend all of your money paying off bad debt if you're not going to rebuild trust along the way.

Imagine that you are a lender. If you had to choose between two people in the following scenario, who would you loan your money to? Person A only shows bad history that's been paid off. Person B has bad history but you see that this person has established new credit history and they have been paying on it very well for over a year. Although both of these people have bad credit, you would feel more comfortable making a loan to person B because they are demonstrating that they are rebuilding their credit.

Chapter 2 – Establishing Good Credit

Secured credit cards are one of the best tools that people can use to rebuild their credit. They are easy to get if you already have bad credit. The concept behind secured credit cards is a straightforward one. You deposit money into a bank account that you will not have access too. In return, the bank gives you a credit card with a limit that is equal to the amount of your deposit. They are protected if you don't make payments because they will simply take your deposit and use it to pay off your credit card if you stop paying on it. It is a no lose situation for the lender. In addition, your payment history will be reported to all three credit bureaus. This will help improve your credit.

The top two banks that offer secured credit cards are Bank of America and Wells Fargo. There is an additional advantage to getting a secured credit card with these two banks. Usually after you have demonstrated good payment history for at least a year, they will graduate your secured card to an unsecured credit card. This means that you will get your deposit back and still be allowed to keep your credit card. There are other banks that do this well such as U.S. Bank, but this is not common. Secured credit cards have annual fees and very high interest rates. This is the cost of rebuilding your credit.

I recommend that you obtain at least three secured credit cards. One of these cards should have at least $1,000 or more as a credit limit. This will show that you can be responsible with a higher credit limit. It is important that you make your payments on time. You should also make sure that you are using less than 30% of your credit limit on each secured credit card. For example, if your limit is $1,000, your balance should be less than $300. When you calculate 30% of $1,000, the result is $300.

It is also important to have a balance on your credit cards. If you keep your balance at 0, then you won't have a payment history. Having a small balance will show payment history.

You can research other secured credit cards besides banks. I am not a big supporter of other secured credit cards because they don't offer graduation programs. The terms of those cards will stay the same. If you go online and search for secured credit cards, you will come across numerous companies that offer these types of cards.

There are also other credit card companies who are not secured credit card companies but specialize in offering cards to people with bad or little credit. It is important that you do your own research on this as well. You can simply go to Google or any other search engine and type in credit cards for bad credit and you will see a list of companies who specialize in this. The following are several of many companies that offer credit cards for people with bad credit; Credit One Bank, First Premiere Bank, First Progress Bank and sometimes Capital One. If your credit is horrendous, you may only qualify for a secured credit card.

Chapter 3 – Managing Your Credit

Once you receive at least three to five credit cards, make sure that you use them responsibly. Keep your balance at 30% or lower of your limit and make you payments on time. This is important to do before you pay off bad debt. This will allow your credit to show good credit instead of only showing bad credit. This is why it is important to get a copy of your credit report before you start working on your credit. You will be informed as to what's on your credit report.

The next important information for you to know is a term called credit inquiry. An inquiry is a record that is placed on your credit report to show what company had access to your credit report. When you apply for a credit card or loan you, an inquiry will be placed on your credit report. Having too many inquires does not help your credit. This is more important when you have rebuilt your credit or if you have good credit. If you're in the process of rebuilding your credit, then inquiries are unavoidable as you attempt to reestablish credit.

Credit reports usually list inquiries within the last 24 months. If you are trying to rebuild your credit, then you will receive a lot of inquiries on your credit report when you are applying for different credit cards.   After you have received the cards that you want, then it's best not to apply for more credit cards. For example, if you have 10 inquiries on your credit report, those inquiries will look worse if they have been recent. Inquiries have a lower impact on your credit score as they age. Eventually, they will be removed from your credit report. It may be a good idea to apply for as many credit inquiries as possible before you stop obtaining inquiries.

Sometimes, inquiries are unavoidable. For example, if you move into a new residence, service providers will place an inquiry on your credit report. The providers are companies such as electric, cable and other types of companies. Don't let having an inquiry stress you out. They go away over a period of time. Their effect will be less as a higher time period passes by.

When you access your own credit report such as through Credit Karma or one of the credit bureaus, these inquiries does not harm your credit. The only inquiries that count against you are when you apply for new credit. There is one important note to mention about inquiries. If you get a large number of inquiries when applying for certain types of credit, it will not affect you as much. For example, if you are shopping for a car loan and 10 lenders pull your credit, it will only hurt your credit as if one or two lenders pulled it. Creditors understand that when people are shopping for cars or homes, they often will look at multiple options. This only applies if you are getting the inquiries within a 2 week period.

The inquiries are usually placed on one or more of the major credit bureaus. There are three major credit bureaus. They are Experian, Equifax and TransUnion. Sometimes one credit bureau may have more information than another. Most lenders and banks will usually use one or more of these three major credit bureaus. It is in your best interest to get a credit report that shows all three credit bureaus. Sometimes one credit bureau may show a bad credit item such as a judgment or lien while another one won't show it. It's best for you to have a full profile of your credit.

Credit Karma is one of the sources that I mentioned earlier in which you can get a free credit report. They usually only show one credit bureau and usually it's Trans Union. This will not accurately show what is on the other two credit bureaus. It is still a good place to start to get some idea how your credit is looking for free. Usually credit scores from the different bureaus are similar to each other. This means that they are usually within 20 to 30 points of each other. For example, if your credit score with Trans Union is 630, your Equifax score may be 650. For your information, credit scores of 700 and above is considered excellent credit. Scores of 630 through 699 is considered good credit. Scores 600-630 is considered fair credit. Bad credit is under 600.

Lenders make their own determination as to what scores they will lend on. Knowing your scores will give you some idea of where your credit standing is. Federal law allows you to have one free detailed credit report from each credit bureau once a year. You are also entitled to a free copy of your credit report if you have been denied credit. You can get your free credit report by going to Annual Credit Report at www.annualcreditreport.com.   You can also go to each of the three major credit bureaus and request your free annual credit report. Usually they all redirect you to Annual Credit Report to obtain this free annual credit report.

Chapter 4 – Time and Management Factor

The most important thing to remember when rebuilding your credit is that it will take time. There are a lot of "repair your credit overnight" companies out there. It's up to you if you wish to try them for yourself. I have tried them and I found that the more patient traditional method of rebuilding your credit works better than "repairing credit overnight." Some of these companies do have an advantage however. For example, some of them write letters to all the lenders who have inquiries on your credit report. If those lenders don't respond in time, those inquiries come off. Most of these companies charge fees. It is important to remember that this alone will not improve your credit. You still have to do the other items that were addressed earlier. Those things include having a good payment history and having at least three credit cards.

There is no big mystery to rebuilding your credit. The main thing to keep in mind is to think like a lender. Ask yourself who you would trust lending your money to if you only saw the details of the person's credit history.

Another important item on your credit report is called credit utilization. Utilization is a number that shows what percentage of your credit limit you are using. For example, if your credit limit is $500 and you are using $50 of this limit, then your utilization percentage is 10 per cent. In order to calculate your utilization is take your balance and divide it by your total credit limit. The number that you get after doing this calculation will show your credit utilization. An easy way manage your utilization is multiply your credit limit 30 percent. The result that you see will show you the target balance to stay below. For example, if your credit limit is $1000 and you multiply that by 30%, the answer is $300. This means that you should keep your balance under $300.

The reason that 30% utilization is the number that you want to stay below is because when your balance exceeds 30% utilization, your credit score gets negatively impacted. As your utilization increases toward 100%, your credit rating will become more negatively impacted.

Think about what utilization means in simple terms. If you are looking at two people and you are trying to determine which one to lend your money too, look at the following scenario. Who would you feel comfortable with lending your money to? Person A is only using 10 percent of their credit limit. Person B is maxing out their entire credit limit. Person A is a better choice because their lower utilization shows that they are using their credit responsibly. It also shows that they are not in danger of financial hardship. If a person is using close to a 100% of the utilization, lenders will think that this person is going through a potential hardship.

The reason why utilization is such a huge factor on your credit is because the lenders have the following view on high utilization. When someone is having financial problems, they start to use a higher percentage of their credit cards to help cover expenses and bills. If they are not using a high percentage of their credit limit, then this means that they are most likely in a financial good position. This is why you must think like a lender.

It is also important to make sure that you are making your payments on time. Usually companies don't report late payments until you are 30 days past your due date. You have some breathing room when it comes to avoiding late payments being reported to your credit history. On a detailed credit report, you will notice that there are three things that show up on the each credit item. It shows how many times you were 30 days, 60 days, and 90 days late. Think about that for a moment. 30 days late means that you are 30 days past your due date.

You can set up reminders on your calendar to help you make your payments on time. You can also choose to bank with a bank that has an online bill payment option and you can set up automatic payments to be sent out on the due dates of your bills. Sometimes people fall behind on their payments on time because they are not paying attention to their due dates. They bury their heads in the sand and just hope it goes away. This is not very responsible. Sometimes people don't think about their credit until they need to use it. It is better to stay on top of your credit so that it's available when you actually need it.

The steps that have been mentioned are easy steps if you remind yourself to think like a lender. The hardest part is actually applying what you've learned. When you develop a routine with applying these steps, then improving your credit will become easier to achieve. After you have your good credit lines established, then your focus should be making your monthly payments on time. Everything else will take care of itself. You also need to make a conscious effort to keep your utilization below 30 percent. If you are having a financially difficult time, then that doesn't have to set your credit back. If you have to increase your utilization, then make payments toward paying it down when you are financially back on track.

Bad debt can be a source of stress for many people. Don't stress out about paying off your bad debt. Some people become emotional when it comes to getting bad debt out of their lives. They start to become focused on paying off debt as quickly and as fast as possible without establishing good credit at the same time. If you pay off all of your bad debt, it does not improve your credit unless you have good credit working for you at the same time. The best way to manage paying off debt is to make sure that you are saving money as you are paying off your debt and making on time payments on your good credit items. When you increase your cash savings while paying down your debt, this will help you stay financially balanced. In the alternative, if you spend all of your money paying down debt and you are left with no cash, this puts you in a position to have to max out your credit if you get into a financial hardship.

End Summary

In conclusion, this book summarizes some strategies and techniques to help get your credit on the right track. It also provides basic understanding as to the different factors that affect your credit. These items are presented in a way to help you put yourself in the shoes of a lender so you can see how they would view your credit. These are simple easy steps that you can take to help improve your credit.

www.ingramcontent.com/pod-product-compliance
Lightning Source LLC
Chambersburg PA
CBHW051423170526
45165CB00004BA/1945